"A Tapestry Of The Roots And Branches Of Our Family"

The descendants and ancestors
of
James Nelson Mewborn
and Marian Verna Fox

Table of Contents

Table of Contents

Descendants of James Nelson Moore

First Generation

1. James Nelson Moore, son of **George Nelson Moore** and **Ida May Billings,** was born on 19 Nov 1913 in Manila, Mississippi County Arkansas, died on 27 Nov 1962 in Memphis, Shelby County Tennessee at age 49, and was buried in Manila Cemetery.

James Nelson Moore snd Marian

James married **Marian Verna Fox,** daughter of **Vernon Richard Fox** and **Clara Augusta Pogue,**. Marian was born on 18 Dec 1913 in Crittenden County Kentucky, died on 25 Jul 1999 in Greeley, Weld County, Colorado at age 85, and was buried in Manila Cemetery.

Children from this marriage were:

+ 2 M   i.   **James Nelson Moore Jr** was born on 26 Nov 1933 in Manila, Mississippi County Arkansas and died on 23 Sep 1983 in Denver Colorado at age 49.

+ 3 M   ii.   **Robert Garrad Moore** was born on 23 Feb 1937 in Manila, Mississippi County Arkansas.

      Robert married **Virginia Ann Johnson** on 17 Jul 1959 in Little Rock, Pulaski County, Arkansas.

+ 4 M   iii.   **Richard Marion Moore** was born on 23 Feb 1937 in Manila, Mississippi County Arkansas.

+ 5 F   iv.   **Brenda Kathryn Moore** was born on 6 Sep 1941 in Blytheville, Mississippi County, Arkansas.

Marian Verna Fox Moore

Brenda married **Walter Bradsher Mewborn** (d. 4 Nov 2008) on 25 Dec 1960 in Somerville, Fayette County, Tennessee.

Second Generation

2. James Nelson Moore Jr *(James Nelson [1])* was born on 26 Nov 1933 in Manila, Mississippi County Arkansas and died on 23 Sep 1983 in Denver Colorado at age 49.

3. Robert Garrad Moore *(James Nelson [1])* was born on 23 Feb 1937 in Manila, Mississippi County Arkansas.

Robert married **Virginia Ann Johnson,** daughter of **Uriel Lee Johnson** and **Charlene Montine McMahan,** on 17 Jul 1959 in Little Rock, Pulaski County, Arkansas. Virginia was born on 12 Feb 1941 in Little Rock, Pulaski County, Arkansas.

4. Richard Marion Moore *(James Nelson [1])* was born on 23 Feb 1937 in Manila, Mississippi County Arkansas.

5. Brenda Kathryn Moore *(James Nelson [1])* was born on 6 Sep 1941 in Blytheville, Mississippi County, Arkansas.

Brenda K. Moore Mewborn

Brenda married **Walter Bradsher Mewborn,** son of **William Gordon Mewborn** and **Eula Elizabeth Bradsher,** on 25 Dec 1960 in Somerville, Fayette County, Tennessee. Walter was born on 19 Nov 1939 in Shelby County Tennessee, died on 4 Nov 2008 in Fayette County Tennessee at age 68, and was buried in Fayette County Memorial Park.

Children from this marriage were:

+ 6 F i. **Melinda Lyn Mewborn** was born on 29 Jan 1962 in Knoxville, Knox County Tennessee.

Melinda married **Robert Michael Franklin** on 27 Aug 1982 in Memphis, Shelby County Tennessee.

+ 7 F ii. **Terri Ann Mewborn** was born on 20 Jun 1963 in Knoxville, Knox County Tennessee.

Terri married **Alpheus Robert Kelley II** on 4 Dec 1982 in Memphis, Shelby County Tennessee.

Terri next married **Robert Cephus White** on 14 May 1994.

Walter B. Mewborn

Descendants of James Nelson Moore

Third Generation

6. Melinda Lyn Mewborn *(Brenda Kathryn Moore [2], James Nelson [1])* was born on 29 Jan 1962 in Knoxville, Knox County Tennessee.

Melinda married **Robert Michael Franklin** on 27 Aug 1982 in Memphis, Shelby County Tennessee. Robert was born on 23 Jan 1958 in Memphis, Shelby County Tennessee.

The child from this marriage was:
+ 8 F   i.   **Leah Michelle Franklin** was born on 20 May 2002 in Memphis, Shelby County Tennessee.

Melinda, Terri, Brenda and Walter

7. Terri Ann Mewborn *(Brenda Kathryn Moore [2], James Nelson [1])* was born on 20 Jun 1963 in Knoxville, Knox County Tennessee.

Terri married **Alpheus Robert Kelley II** on 4 Dec 1982 in Memphis, Shelby County Tennessee. Alpheus was born on 28 Apr 1958.

Children from this marriage were:
+ 9 F   i.   **Kristen Leigh Kelley** was born on 11 May 1986 in Memphis, Shelby County Tennessee.

+ 10 F   ii.   **Katelyn Ann Kelley** was born on 6 Sep 1989 in Memphis, Shelby County Tennessee.

Terri next married **Robert Cephus White** on 14 May 1994. Robert was born on 7 May 1956.

Fourth Generation

8. Leah Michelle Franklin *(Melinda Lyn Mewborn [3], Brenda Kathryn Moore [2], James Nelson [1])* was born on 20 May 2002 in Memphis, Shelby County Tennessee.

9. Kristen Leigh Kelley *(Terri Ann Mewborn [3], Brenda Kathryn Moore [2], James Nelson [1])* was born on 11 May 1986 in Memphis, Shelby County Tennessee.

10. Katelyn Ann Kelley *(Terri Ann Mewborn [3], Brenda Kathryn Moore [2], James Nelson [1])* was born on 6 Sep 1989 in Memphis, Shelby County Tennessee.

First Generation

1. James Nelson Moore, son of **George Nelson Moore** and **Ida May Billings,** was born on 19 Nov 1913 in Manila, Mississippi County Arkansas, died on 27 Nov 1962 in Memphis, Shelby County Tennessee at age 49, and was buried in Manila Cemetery.

James Nelson Moore snd Marian

James married **Marian Verna Fox,** daughter of **Vernon Richard Fox** and **Clara Augusta Pogue,**.

Children from this marriage were:

    i.   **James Nelson Moore Jr** was born on 26 Nov 1933 in Manila, Mississippi County Arkansas and died on 23 Sep 1983 in Denver Colorado at age 49.

    ii.   **Robert Garrad Moore** was born on 23 Feb 1937 in Manila, Mississippi County Arkansas.

    iii.   **Richard Marion Moore** was born on 23 Feb 1937 in Manila, Mississippi County Arkansas.

    iv.   **Brenda Kathryn Moore** was born on 6 Sep 1941 in Blytheville, Mississippi County, Arkansas.

Marian Verna Fox Moore

Second Generation (Parents)

2. George Nelson Moore, son of **Nelson Moore** and **Caroline Jones,** was born on 22 Dec 1881 in Garrard County Kentucky, died on 31 May 1918 in Manila, Mississippi County, Arkansas at age 36, and was buried in Manila Cemetery.

General Notes: Died at Baptist Hospital Memphis of Stomach Cancer

George married **Ida May Billings** on 5 Jul 1903 in Maniila, Mississippi County Arkansas.

Marriage Notes: Arkansas, County Marriages Index, 1837-1957 about G N Moore
Name: G N Moore
Residence: Manila, Arkansas
Spouse's Name: Ida Billings
Spouse's Residence: Manila, Arkansas
Marriage Date: 5 Jul 1903
Event Type: Marriage Bond
FHL Film Number: 1302581

Children from this marriage were:

- i.   **Mollie Moore** was born on 29 Sep 1906 in Mississippi County Arkansas, died on 27 Mar 1993 in Manila, Mississippi County Arkansas at age 86, and was buried in Manila Cemetery.

1   ii.   **James Nelson Moore**

- iii.   **Samuel Wesley Moore** was born in 1916 in Mississippi County Arkansas.

- iv.   **Roy V. Moore** was born in 1918 in Mississippi County Arkansas.

George Nelson - Ida (Billings)Moore & Mollie

3. Ida May Billings, daughter of **Spruce Wesley Billings** and **Mary Elizabeth Davis,** was born on 12 Aug 1884 in Tipton County Tennessee, died on 6 Nov 1931 in Manila, Mississippi County Arkansas at age 47, and was buried in Manila Cemetery.

Ida married **George Nelson Moore** on 5 Jul 1903 in Maniila, Mississippi County Arkansas.

Ida next married **Carl Lay.**

Third Generation (Grandparents)

4. Nelson Moore, son of **Samuel R. Moore** and **Nancy Jane Moore,** was born circa 1855 in Hawkins County Tennessee and died before 1885 in Big Lake, Mississippi County Arkansas. The cause of his death was Committed Suicide.

Nelson married **Caroline Jones** on 28 Dec 1879 in Lee County Arkansas.

Marriage Notes: Arkansas, County Marriages Index, 1837-1957 about Nelson Moore
Name: Nelson Moore
Age: 24
Birth Year: abt 1855
Spouse's Name: Caroline Jones
Spouse's Age: 19
Marriage Date: 28 Dec 1879
Marriage License Date: 26 Dec 1879
Marriage County: Lee
Event Type: Marriage
FHL Film Number: 1017652

The child from this marriage was:

2   i.   **George Nelson Moore**

5. Caroline Jones, daughter of **Stephen Hampton Jones** and **Elizabeth Bethina Jones,** was born circa 1849 in Pickens County Alabama and died circa 1910 in Big Lake, Mississippi County Arkansas about age 61.

Caroline married **Nelson Moore** on 28 Dec 1879 in Lee County Arkansas.

Caroline next married **L. Newton Ashabranner** on 19 Aug 1888 in Big Lake, Mississippi County Arkansas.

6. Spruce Wesley Billings, son of **James Abner Billings** and **Nancy Elizabeth Roe,** was born about 1861 in Tipton County Tennessee, died on 25 Aug 1936 in Mississippi County Arkansas about age 75, and was buried in Manila Cemetery.

Spruce married **Mary Elizabeth Davis** on 2 Dec 1879 in Tipton County Tennessee.

The child from this marriage was:

> 3   i.   **Ida May Billings**

7. Mary Elizabeth Davis, daughter of **John M. Davis** and **Mary Ann Marshall,** was born on 7 Apr 1861 in Tipton County Tennessee and died on 11 Apr 1898 in Tipton County Tennessee at age 37.

Mary married **Spruce Wesley Billings** on 2 Dec 1879 in Tipton County Tennessee.

Fourth Generation (Great-Grandparents)

8. Samuel R. Moore, son of **Zodac Moore** and **Barbara Aft,** was born in 1818 in Hawkins County Tennessee and died after 1890 in Hawkins County Tennessee.

> General Notes: 30 North Carolina Infantry
>
> 30th Regiment, North Carolina Infantry Conf.
> 30th Infantry Regiment completed its organization at Camp Mangum, near Raleigh, North Carolina, in October, 1861. The men were raised in the following counties: Sampson, Warren, Brunswick, Wake, Nash, Granville, Duplin, Edgecombe, Moore, and Mecklenburg. It served in the Department of North Carolina, then was assigned to General G.B. Anderson's, Ramseur's, and Cox's Brigade, Army of Northern Virginia. The 30th saw action from Seven Pines to Cold Harbor, marched with Early to the Shenandoah Valley, and was involved in the Appomattox operations. The unit reported 30 killed and 137 wounded during the Seven Days' Battles, lost thirty-six percent of the 250 in the Maryland Campaign, and had 9 wounded at Fredericksburg. It sustained 125 casualties at Chancellorsville, lost sixteen percent of the 278 engaged at Gettysburg, and had 3 killed and 42 wounded on the Rappahannock River. On April 9, 1865, it surrendered 6 officers and 147 men. The field officers wre Colonel Francis M. Parker; Lieutenant Colonels Walter Draughan, James T. Kell, and William W. Sillers; and Major James C. Holmes.

Samuel married **Nancy Jane Moore**.

The child from this marriage was:

> 4   i.   **Nelson Moore**

9. Nancy Jane Moore, daughter of **Unknown** and **Elizabeth Moore,** was born in 1823 in Hawkins County Tennessee and died after 1880 in Hawkins County Tennessee.

Nancy married **Samuel R. Moore**.

10. Stephen Hampton Jones, son of **Robert Jones** and **Elizabeth,** was born on 15 Oct 1819 in Laurens District South Carolina and died on 6 Sep 1858 in Pickens County Alabama at age 38.

Stephen married **Elizabeth Bethina Jones** on 24 Dec 1848 in Pickens County Alabama.

The child from this marriage was:

> 5   i.   **Caroline Jones**

11. Elizabeth Bethina Jones, daughter of **Hezekiah Jones** and **Elizabeth "Betsy" McGowen,** was born on 31 Mar 1824 in Pickens County Alabama and died on 5 Aug 1906 in Choctaw County Mississippi at age 82.

Elizabeth married **Stephen Hampton Jones** on 24 Dec 1848 in Pickens County Alabama.

12. James Abner Billings, son of **David Billings** and **Susannah Macay,** was born on 9 Apr 1830 in Linclon County Tennessee and died on 5 Mar 1887 in Tipton County Tennessee at age 56.

> General Notes: James A. Billings

James A. Billings, farmer and merchant of the Third District, is a son of David and Susan Ann (McCoy) Billings. He was born in Lincoln County in 1830, and is the sixth child of a family of fifteen children -- seven sons and eight daughters; four sons and three daughters living. The father was of German ancestry, born in North Carolina in 1794. He was raised in his native State, and married when about twenty-five years old, and moved to Lincoln County in 1825, farming there until 1837, when he moved to Tipton County and located near what is now the Twelfth District, where he died in 1851, being one of the early settlers. The mother was born in North Carolina in 1802 and died in 1858. Our subject was raised and educated in Tipton County. November, 1855, he married Nancy E., daughter of John and Sallie Roe. They had sixteen children -- four sons and four daughters living: Lucy Ann (wife of M. A. Phillips), Margaret, Elizabeth Jennie, Mary Matilda, James Henry, Spruce, Holmes Cummings, and Pink. Mr. Billings spent a year after his marriage in the Twelfth District, then moved to his present farm, owning about 400 acres of land in different tracts; 124 acres in the home tract is well cultivated and is nine miles west of Covington, near Walnut Grove Church. In 1874 he purchased a stock of goods and since then has been engaged in the mercantile business in connection with his farming. He is a good business man, and was elected magistrate in 1876, holding the office for six years. He is a firm Democrat. Mrs. Billings was born in Lincoln County in 1838, and is a member of the Methodist Episcopal Church South.

Goodspeed's History of Tennessee (1887)

James married **Nancy Elizabeth Roe** on 20 Nov 1855 in Tipton County Tennessee.

The child from this marriage was:

> 6   i.   **Spruce Wesley Billings**

13. Nancy Elizabeth Roe, daughter of **John Roe** and **Sarah Sallie Alice Pendergrass,** was born on 2 Oct 1838 in Lincoln County Tennessee and died on 18 Jun 1896 in Tipton County Tennessee at age 57.

Nancy married **James Abner Billings** on 20 Nov 1855 in Tipton County Tennessee.

14. John M. Davis, son of **Thomas Davis** and **Nancy Ann Lampkin,** was born circa 1818 in Polk County Tennessee and died before 1880 in Tipton County Tennessee.

John married **Mary Ann Marshall** circa 1839.

Children from this marriage were:

> 7   i.   **Mary Elizabeth Davis**
>
> ii.   **Charles Davis** was born in Apr 1854 in Tipton County Tennessee.

15. Mary Ann Marshall, daughter of **William Marshall** and **Martha,** was born circa 1821 in Shelby County Tennessee The Part that became Tipton Co. and died after 1880 in Tipton County Tennessee.

> General Notes: Listed as widow in 1880 Tipton Co.

> D.L. Davis Child of Mary and John M's died in 1921 5-5 states his mothers name is Mary Ann Marshall

Mary married **John M. Davis** circa 1839.

Fifth Generation (Great Great-Grandparents)

16. Zodac Moore, son of **Thomas Moore** and **Roseannah Fowler,** was born on 9 Jan 1775 in Greenville Dist South Carolina, died on 18 Mar 1844 in Hawkins County Tennessee at age 69, and was buried in Keele Cemetery Bulls Gap TN.

Grave stone of Zadoc Moore

General Notes: March 19, 1844

In the name of God, Amen. I Zadock Moore of the County of Hawkins and State of Tennessee, being in bad state of health but of sound mind and memory do make this my last Will and Testament in the words following, that is to say. I want all my funeral and burial expenses paid and all my just debts that is against me. I will and bequeath to my dear wife Barbary Moore all my household and kitchen furniture and peaceable & uninterrupted possession of the house & all the buildings as for as she may need and the profits and rents of the land belonging to me, as much at least as she may need for a decent support with the exception of what may be needed hereafter. I want her to have a gentle horse to ride and two milk cows of her own choosing of the cows that belong to me and the clock now in the house and plow and pair of work gears and singletree and clevis. I want the wagon and gearing to remain on the farm for the use of the same and all the hodges belonging to me and sufficienty of the grain on the farm belonging to me for her support this year, and also one third of the wheat that is growing and the catring and flax wheels and the real and one side saddle and riding bridle and all the sheep and all my books. I want my son William Moore to take my sorrel horse named Challey and trade her in any way so as to get such a horse as named in the will for the use of his mother. I want Susannah McCullough to have uninterrupted possession of the house where she now lives and have the same privileges for support as she has heretofore had, during her lifetime. I want at the death of my before named wife, all the property sold and equally divided between the heirs of my daughter Susannah Moore, dec'd and my daughter Rosannah Phillips & my daughter Ann Cane Bogart and the heirs of my daughter Winnea Keele, dec'd., and it is my will that John Rogers, William Shepherd and Isaac Phillips lay off to Thomas Moore my son, one third in value and in land of the place where I now live in satisfaction of his Deed made by Micajah Lee to him. And the above named vallueners is not to take the improvement that said Moore has made as any part of the value of said land, and the said valluenes is to lay off said land on the upper part of the tract so as to include his improvements and clear across the plantation the land to be valluered according to quality and quantity. And at the death of my wife as above named the balance of the land is to be equally divided between my three sons, William, Thomas and Samuel R. according to quality and quantity. The personal property not named in the will, after my death is the be sold, my debts as above named paid. The balance of any of said sale is to go to the use of my wife. I want William and Thomas Moore Executors of this my last will. This 19th day of March, 1844.
Zadok Moore Test.
Martin Phillips, James Moore

Wills of Hawkins County Tennessee
Published by the Hawkins County Genealogical & Historical Society, 1991

Seven children have been identified:
Ann Moore
Rosannah L. Moore
Susannah Moore
Winnoa Moore
William Moore
Thomas Moore
Samuel R. Moore

Zodac married **Barbara Aft** in 1808 in Tennessee.

The child from this marriage was:

8   i.   **Samuel R. Moore**

17. Barbara Aft was born on 21 Nov 1794 in Tennessee, died on 3 Sep 1849 in Hamblin County Tennessee at age 54, and was buried in Keele Cemetery Bulls Gap TN.

Barbara married **Zodac Moore** in 1808 in Tennessee.

19. Elizabeth Moore, daughter of **Jesse Moore** and **Unknown,** was born in 1801 in Tennessee and died after 1860 in Hawkins County Tennessee.

Elizabeth married someone.

Her child was:

> 9   i.   **Nancy Jane Moore**

20. Robert Jones was born in 1772 in South Carolina and died after 1860 in Pickens County Alabama.

Robert married **Elizabeth** before 1809 in Laurens District South Carolina.

The child from this marriage was:

> 10   i.   **Stephen Hampton Jones**

21. Elizabeth was born in 1777 in South Carolina and died after 1860 in Pickens County Alabama.

Elizabeth married **Robert Jones** before 1809 in Laurens District South Carolina.

22. Hezekiah Jones was born on 21 Jul 1789 in Caswell County North Carolina and died on 5 Apr 1855 in Pickens County Alabama at age 65.

Hezekiah married **Elizabeth "Betsy" McGowen** on 29 Dec 1814 in Pickens County Alabama.

The child from this marriage was:

> 11   i.   **Elizabeth Bethina Jones**

23. Elizabeth "Betsy" McGowen was born on 21 May 1797 and died on 5 Oct 1863 in Pickens County Alabama at age 66.

Elizabeth married **Hezekiah Jones** on 29 Dec 1814 in Pickens County Alabama.

24. David Billings, son of **Dr. John Siegfried (Johannes) Billings** and **Julianna Weller,** was born in 1794 in Rowan County North Carolina and died in 1855 in Tipton County Tennessee at age 61.

David married **Susannah Macay**.

The child from this marriage was:

> 12   i.   **James Abner Billings**

25. Susannah Macay was born in 1802 in Rowan County North Carolina and died in 1858 in Tipton County Tennessee at age 56.

Susannah married **David Billings**.

26. John Roe, son of **Samuel Roe** and **Nancy Sturgeon,** was born on 11 Jul 1819 in Lincoln County Tennessee, died on 13 Aug 1853 in Tipton County Tennessee at age 34, and was buried in Shiloh Cemetery.

John married **Sarah Sallie Alice Pendergrass** in Lincoln County Tennessee.

The child from this marriage was:

    13   i.   **Nancy Elizabeth Roe**

Grave of John Roe

27. Sarah Sallie Alice Pendergrass was born on 16 Jul 1819, died on 6 Nov 1875 in Tipton County Tennessee at age 56, and was buried in Shiloh Cemetery.

Sarah married **John Roe** in Lincoln County Tennessee.

Grave of Sarah Alice Roe

28. Thomas Davis, son of **Moses Davis** and **Jean (or Jane) Noble,** was born about 1794 in Abbeville District South Carolina and died on 9 Oct 1866 in Sturgis, Oktibbeha County Mississippi about age 72.

    General Notes: 1840 Census: Thomas Davis has listed Males: 3 under 5 yrs, 2 at 20-30 yrs,1 male 30-40yrs, 2 males 40-50yrs, 1 female 5-10yrs, 1 female 10-15 yrs, 1 female 20-30yrs., 1 female 40-50 yrs. (page 121 on Oktibbeha County Census.

    1850 Census: Thomas Davis is #187. Thomas is 58 yrs old, listed as farmer, worth is $5,000, wife is Nancy, age 50, son John is 32 yrs, Sissania, age 20 yrs, William is 11 yrs. Also in the household is William Lampkin, age 56, farmer from South Carolina, Hamilton Turner 22 yrs old, farmer, Dr. J.M. Bond, physician born in Tennessee, Chaney Bishop, aged 100 yrs, listed as black. Brother Robert Davis is # 188

    1860 Slave Registry lists Thomas Davis as owning 60 slaves.

    From " The History Of Pickens County, Alabama" by J.F. Clanahan, page 179.... " The third sherrif of Pickens County was

Thomas Davis, who came from Abbeyville District, South Carolina first to Kentucky, then to Margengo County, and on to Pickens about 1819. He married a Lampkin. He was elected sheriff in 1826 and served out his term. Mr. Davis also lived in the Yorkville area. Soon after going out of office, Mr. Davis moved to Choctaw County, Mississippi."

More About Thomas Davis:
Burial: Unknown, Family graves in Morgantown, Mississippi.

Thomas married **Nancy Ann Lampkin**.

The child from this marriage was:

    14   i.   **John M. Davis**

29. Nancy Ann Lampkin was born in 1800 in South Carolina and died on 10 Jul 1865 in Sturgis , Oktibbeha County, Mississippi at age 65.

Nancy married **Thomas Davis**.

30. William Marshall was born between 1780 and 1790 and died before 1850 in Tipton County Tennessee.

William married **Martha**.

The child from this marriage was:

    15   i.   **Mary Ann Marshall**

31. Martha was born in Dec 1800 in North Carolina.

Martha married **William Marshall**.

Sixth Generation (3rd Great-Grandparents)

32. Thomas Moore was born on 4 Aug 1739 in Ireland, died on 22 Nov 1833 in Knox County Kentucky at age 94, and was buried in Lynn Camp Cemetery Gray Knox County Kentucky.

Thomas married **Roseannah Fowler** in 1764 in Laurens District South Carolina.

Children from this marriage were:

    16   i.   **Zodac Moore**

           ii.   **Ephraim Moore**

          iii.   **Joab Moore**

          iv.   **Jesse Moore**

Grave stone of Thomas Moore born in Ireland

33. Roseannah Fowler was born on 22 Aug 1747 in Jefferson County Kentucky and died in Feb 1803 in Knox County Kentucky at age 55.

Roseannah married **Thomas Moore** in 1764 in Laurens District South Carolina.

ROSANNA MOORE
1747 — 1833

Grave of Rosanna (Fowler) Moore

38. Jesse Moore, son of **Thomas Moore** and **Roseannah Fowler,**.

Jesse married someone.

His child was:

    19   i.   **Elizabeth Moore**

48. Dr. John Siegfried (Johannes) Billings, son of **Willhelm Siegfried Billings** and **Phillipina Margaretta Frenck,** was born on 10 Nov 1730 in Anspach, now Ansbach, Bavaria, Germany and died circa 1801 in Rowan County North Carolina about age 71.

    General Notes: BILLINGS, JOHN SIEGFRIED Ancestor #: A087594 DAR Patriot Index
    Service: NORTH CAROLINA   Rank: PATRIOTIC SERVICE
    Birth: 11-1-1730   ANSBACH GERMANY
    Death: 1-30-1801   ROWAN CO NORTH CAROLINA
    Service Description: 1) REIMBURSED FOR SUPPLIES

    Comments (Overview)

    1) SS: NC STATE ARCHIVES, REV ARMY ACCTS VOL VIII P 74 FOLIO 2

    Residence

    1) County: ROWAN CO - State: NORTH CAROLINA

    Spouse
    Number Name
    1) JULIANA WELLER

John married **Julianna Weller** circa 1754.

The child from this marriage was:

    24   i.   **David Billings**

49. Julianna Weller, daughter of **Heinrich Weller** and **Anna Catharina Stegemann,** was born on 28 Jun 1733 in Bavaria, Germany, died on 12 Jan 1804 in Davidson County, NC at age 70, and was buried in Beck Reformed Lutheran Church Cemetery.

Julianna married **Dr. John Siegfried (Johannes) Billings** circa 1754.

52. Samuel Roe, son of **John Sayre Roe** and **Mary Ward,** was born in 1781 in Queen Annes County, Maryland and died on 7 Nov 1865 in Lawrence County Missouri at age 84.

Samuel married **Nancy Sturgeon**.

The child from this marriage was:

    26   i.   **John Roe**

53. Nancy Sturgeon was born in 1792 in South Carolina and died after 1875 in Lawrence County Missouri.

Nancy married **Samuel Roe**.

56. Moses Davis, son of **Robert Davis** and **Unknown,** was born in 1735 in Abbeville District South Carolina and died on 6 Sep 1804 in Abbeville District South Carolina at age 69.

Moses married **Jean (or Jane) Noble** in 1773 in Abbeville District South Carolina.

The child from this marriage was:

    28   i.   **Thomas Davis**

57. Jean (or Jane) Noble, daughter of **John Noble** and **Mary Katherine Calhoun,** was born in 1745 in Lancaster County Pennsylvania and died in Abbeville District South Carolina.

Jean married **Moses Davis** in 1773 in Abbeville District South Carolina.

Seventh Generation (4th Great-Grandparents)

76. Thomas Moore
(Duplicate. See Person 32 on Page 12)

77. Roseannah Fowler
(Duplicate. See Person 33 on Page 12)

96. Willhelm Siegfried Billings.

Willhelm married **Phillipina Margaretta Frenck** before 1730.

The child from this marriage was:

    48   i.   **Dr. John Siegfried (Johannes) Billings**

97. Phillipina Margaretta Frenck.

Phillipina married **Willhelm Siegfried Billings** before 1730.

98. Heinrich Weller was born in 1710 in Germany and died on 3 Jul 1804 in Mettingenm, Esslingen, Baden-Wuerttemberg, Germany at age 94.

Heinrich married **Anna Catharina Stegemann** before 1733 in Mettingenm, Esslingen, Baden-Wuerttemberg, Germany.

The child from this marriage was:

    49   i.   **Julianna Weller**

99. Anna Catharina Stegemann was born on 17 May 1730 in Mettingenm, Esslingen, Baden-Wuerttemberg, Germany and died on 10 Jul 1796 in Mettingenm, Esslingen, Baden-Wuerttemberg, Germany at age 66.

Anna married **Heinrich Weller** before 1733 in Mettingenm, Esslingen, Baden-Wuerttemberg, Germany.

104. John Sayre Roe, son of **Benjamin Roe** and **Elizabeth,** was born circa 1760 in Costal Shores of Maryland, died on 12 Aug 1847 in Smith County Tennessee about age 87, and was buried in Roe-Wilson Cemetery.

Grave of Revolutionary War Soldier John Roe

General Notes: ROWE, JOHN   DAR Ancestor #: A099147
Service: MARYLAND   Rank: DRUMMER
Birth: (CIRCA) 1760   EASTERN SHORE MARYLAND
Death: (ANTE) 12 Aug 1847   SMITH CO TENNESSEE
Service Source: ARCH OF MD, VOL 18, P18
Service Description: 1) MD 9TH CO OF LIGHT INFANTRY CAPT GEORGE STRICKER

Descendants of Thomas Row

1.Thomas Row b: in England d: Bet. 1702 - 1703 in Somerset County, Maryland
. +Ann m: Bef. 1670 in England

Children:

1.THOMAS ROE, Sr. - Born - Abt. 1670
2. Joseph Roe
3. John Roe
4. Nicholas Roe

2. Thomas Roe, Sr. b: Abt. 1670 in Somerset County, Maryland d: Bet. 1711 - 1712 in Queen Anne's County, Maryland
... +Frances

Children:

1. Thomas Roe, Jr.
2. William Roe
3. JOHN ROE d: Bef. August 15, 1737
4. Mary married Mr. Waters
5. Frances married Mr. Lane

3. John Roe d: Bef. August 15, 1737 in Queen Anne's County, Maryland
..... +Martha

Children:

1.THOMAS ROE
2. Edward Roe - married Sarah Richardson
Children:
A. Joseph Roe b: Abt. 1718 in Queen Annes County,
Maryland
B. Samuel Roe b: Abt. 1722 in Queen Annes County, Maryland
C. Thomas Richardson Roe b: Abt. 1724 in Queen Annes County, Maryland
... +Margaret Holton
. D. James Roe b: Bet. January 14, 1742 - 1743 in
Queen Annes County, Maryland
d: September 1789 in Queen Annes County, Maryland Burial: Roe Cemetery,
Caroline County, Maryland
..... +Margaret Sylvester
E. James Roe b: Abt. 1726 in Queen Annes County, Maryland d: Abt. 1768
... +Rachel b: 1730 in Queen Annes County, Maryland m: 1751 in Queen Annes
County, Maryland
F. John Roe b: Abt. 1732 in Queen Annes County, Maryland d: 1783 in Richmond,

North Carolina
G. Rachel Roe b: Abt. 1723 in Kent County, Maryland d: January 20, 1775

4 Thomas Roe b: in Queen Anne's County, Maryland d: Bef. July 22, 1754 in
Queen Anne's County, Maryland
.... +Dinah

Children:

1. BENJAMIN ROE
2. John Roe
3. Elizabeth Roe

5.Benjamin Roe b: in Queen Anne's County, Maryland d: Bef. April 26, 1784
in Queen Anne's County, Maryland
.... +Elizabeth

Children:

1. JOHN SAYRE ROE, SR.

6. John Sayre Roe, Sr. b: 1748 in Queen Anne's County, Maryland d: Bef.
1830 in Smith County, Tennessee Burial: Roe/Wilson Cemetery, Rock
City, Smith County, Tennessee (Has Rev. War Marker) Military Records:
Rev. War Soldier(Drummer)
.... +Mary Ward b: Abt. 1752 in Maryland m: December 23, 1777 in Chas
County, Maryland d: Bef. 1830 in Smith County, Tennessee Burial:
Roe/Wilson Cemetery, Rock City, Smith County, Tennessee

Children:

1. James Roe
2. Nancy Roe
3. Samuel Roe b: 1781 in Maryland d: November 07, 1865 in Lawrence
County,
Missouri
... +Nancy Sturgeon b: 1792 in South Carolina d: 1875 in Lawrence County,
Missouri
4.Thomas Roe

5.Benjamin T. Roe b: 1785 in Tennessee d: February 06, 1834 in Smith County,
Tennessee Burial: Purnell Cemetery, Smith County, Tennessee
... +Mary b: Abt. 1795 in Tennessee d: Bef. 1850 in Smith County, Tennessee
Burial: Probably in unmarked grave in Purnell Cemetery, Smith County,
Tennessee
6.Margaret Roe b: in Maryland
... +William Hodges b: Abt. 1792
7.JOHN SAYRE ROE, JR. b: May 05, 1792 in Queen Anne's County, Maryland d:
August 15, 1856 in Rome, Smith County, Tennessee Burial: Roe/Wilson
Cemetery, Rock City, Smith County, Tennessee
... +Nancy Chandler b: December 25, 1798 in Wattsville, Laurens County, South
Carolina m: December 06, 1819 in Tennessee d: December 25, 1872 in Rome,
Smith County, Tennessee Burial: Roe/Wilson Cemetery, Rock City, Smith
County, Tennessee Father: Josiah Chandler Mother: Sarah (Salley) Eddins
8.Mary Roe b: Abt. 1800 d: Bef. 1847 in Probably Blount County, Alabama
... +Philip Foust b: 1799 in Tennessee

John married **Mary Ward** on 23 Dec 1777 in Charles County, Maryland.

The child from this marriage was:

> 52   i.   **Samuel Roe**

105. Mary Ward was born circa 1760 in Maryland, died circa 1820 in Smith County Tennessee about age 60, and was buried in Roe-Wilson Cemetery.

Mary married **John Sayre Roe** on 23 Dec 1777 in Charles County, Maryland.

112. Robert Davis was born circa 1717 in Ulster Ireland and died in 1773 in Meckenlenburg County North Carolina about age 56.

Robert married someone.

His child was:

> 56   i.   **Moses Davis**

114. John Noble was born about 1714 in Ireland and died in Nov 1752 in Augusta County Virginia about age 38.

John married **Mary Katherine Calhoun** in 1732 in Donegal County , Ireland.

The child from this marriage was:

> 57   i.   **Jean (or Jane) Noble**

115. Mary Katherine Calhoun was born circa 1714 in Donegal County , Ireland and died on 1 Feb 1760 in Abbeville District South Carolina about age 46.

> General Notes: Catherine Calhoun, the only daughter of James Calhoun, the Emigrant and his wife Catherine Montgomery Calhoun was born in Ireland about 1718. She married John Noble in Ireland, (and therefore was evidently not with her parents when they emigrated to American in 1732). She had three children, the eldest of whom Alexander Noble was born at sea as his father and mother came to American. Catherine Calhoun Noble became a widow early in life and made her home with her brothers' families. She and her children escaped the Massacre of Long Cane Creek and settled with other members of the family in Abbeville Distract. Her children were Alexander Noble, James Noble and a daughter whose name is not given:" from NOTABLE SOUTHERN FAMILIES, VOLUMES I & II.
> "Following a 1740 Treaty between the Cherokee Nation and the Province of South Carolina, all lands west and north of Long Cane Creek were closed to settlers. In 1758, the Calhoun Family, of Scotch-Irish decent and fleeing famine and religious persecution, were granted large tracts of land near the boundery. Fearing encroachment by immigrants, the Cherokee, previously friendly, started to launch attacks on settlers. On February 1, 1760, the Calhoun's and others were attacked while in route to Augusta's Fort Moore for protection. There were 32 victims buried in a mass grave. That grave include the grandmother of V.P. John C. Calhoun." From internet on South Carolina History

Mary married **John Noble** in 1732 in Donegal County , Ireland.

Eighth Generation (5th Great-Grandparents)

208. Benjamin Roe, son of **Thomas Roe** and **Dianah,** was born in Queen Annes County, Maryland and died before 26 Apr 1784 in Queen Annes County, Maryland.

Benjamin married **Elizabeth**.

The child from this marriage was:

> 104   i.   **John Sayre Roe**

209. Elizabeth.

Elizabeth married **Benjamin Roe**.

Ninth Generation (6th Great-Grandparents)

416. Thomas Roe, son of **John Roe** and **Martha,** was born in Queen Annes County, Maryland and died before 22 Jul 1754 in Queen Annes County, Maryland.

Thomas married **Dianah**.

The child from this marriage was:

    208   i.   **Benjamin Roe**

417. Dianah.

Dianah married **Thomas Roe**.

Tenth Generation (7th Great-Grandparents)

832. John Roe, son of **Thomas Roe** and **Frances,** died before 15 Aug 1737 in Queen Annes County, Maryland.

John married **Martha**.

The child from this marriage was:

    416   i.   **Thomas Roe**

833. Martha.

Martha married **John Roe**.

11th Generation (8th Great-Grandparents)

1664. Thomas Roe, son of **Thomas Roe** and **Ann,** was born about 1670 in Somerset County, Maryland and died between 1711 and 1712 in Queen Annes County, Maryland.

Thomas married **Frances**.

The child from this marriage was:

    832   i.   **John Roe**

1665. Frances.

Frances married **Thomas Roe**.

12th Generation (9th Great-Grandparents)

3328. Thomas Roe was born in England and died from 1702 to 1703 in Somerset County, Maryland.

Thomas married **Ann** in 1670 in England.

The child from this marriage was:

    1664   i.   **Thomas Roe**

3329. Ann.

Ann married **Thomas Roe** in 1670 in England.

First Generation

1. Marian Verna Fox, daughter of **Vernon Richard Fox** and **Clara Augusta Pogue,** was born on 18 Dec 1913 in Crittenden County Kentucky, died on 25 Jul 1999 in Greeley, Weld County, Colorado at age 85, and was buried in Manila Cemetery.

Marian Verna Fox Moore

Marian married **James Nelson Moore,** son of **George Nelson Moore** and **Ida May Billings,**.

Children from this marriage were:

    i.   **James Nelson Moore Jr** was born on 26 Nov 1933 in Manila, Mississippi County Arkansas and died on 23 Sep 1983 in Denver Colorado at age 49.

    ii.   **Robert Garrad Moore** was born on 23 Feb 1937 in Manila, Mississippi County Arkansas.

    iii.   **Richard Marion Moore** was born on 23 Feb 1937 in Manila, Mississippi County Arkansas.

    iv.   **Brenda Kathryn Moore** was born on 6 Sep 1941 in Blytheville, Mississippi County, Arkansas.

Marian next married **Robert Joseph Wambaugh**.

James Nelson Moore snd Marian

Ancestors of Marian Verna Fox

Second Generation (Parents)

2. Vernon Richard Fox, son of **Charles Wesley Fox** and **Juliet Hodge,** was born on 2 May 1884 in Lebanon, Marion County, Kentucky and died in May 1968 in Manila, Mississippi County Arkansas at age 84.

Vernon married **Clara Augusta Pogue** in 1909 in Crittenden County Kentucky.

Children from this marriage were:

     i.   **Thelma N. Fox** was born on 16 Feb 1911 in Crittenden County Kentucky and died in 1919 in Maniila, Mississippi County Arkansas at age 8.

1   ii.   **Marian Verna Fox**

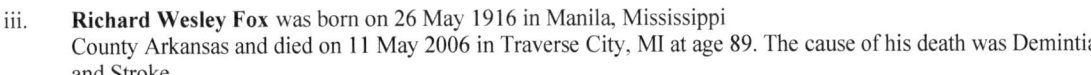
Vernon R. & Children Bill, Bud & Marian

    iii.   **Richard Wesley Fox** was born on 26 May 1916 in Manila, Mississippi County Arkansas and died on 11 May 2006 in Traverse City, MI at age 89. The cause of his death was Demintia and Stroke.

    iv.   **William Garrad Fox** was born on 21 Aug 1918 in Manila, Mississippi County, Arkansas and died on 14 Nov 2007 in Lenoir City, Loudon County, Tennessee at age 89.

3. Clara Augusta Pogue, daughter of **Marion Forrest Pogue** and **Bettie Florence Matthews,** was born on 12 May 1888 in Crittenden County Kentucky and died in Aug 1936 in Manila, Mississippi County Arkansas at age 48.

Noted events in her life were:
• Cause of Death: colon cancer.

Clara married **Vernon Richard Fox** in 1909 in Crittenden County Kentucky.

Clara A. Pogue Fox

Third Generation (Grandparents)

4. Charles Wesley Fox, son of **John Wesley Fox** and **Elizabeth King,** was born on 9 Sep 1857 in Cincinatti, Hamilton County Ohio, died on 27 Aug 1927 in Livingston, Crittenden County, Kentucky at age 69, and was buried in Owens Cemetery.

Charles married **Juliet Hodge** on 8 Sep 1881 in Crittenden County, Kentucky.

The child from this marriage was:

    2   i.   **Vernon Richard Fox**

5. Juliet Hodge, daughter of **Asel Branson Hodge** and **Catharine Elizabeth Millikan,** was born on 18 Apr 1860 in Crittenden County, Kentucky, died on 20 Apr 1925 in Crittenden County, Kentucky at age 65, and was buried in Owens Cemetery.

Juliet married **Charles Wesley Fox** on 8 Sep 1881 in Crittenden County, Kentucky.

6. Marion Forrest Pogue, son of **William Washington Pogue** and **Mary Catherine Oliver,** was born on 18 Oct 1867 in Crittenden County Kentucky, died on 26 Sep 1952 in Caldwell County Kentucky at age 84, and was buried in Frances Presbyterian Church Cemetery Frances Crittenden County Kentucky.

> General Notes: M.F. POGUE
> Representative Seventh District
> MARION FORREST POGUE Representative Seventh District Fredonia Crittenden county District Crittenden and Livingston counties Democrat Farmer merchant Born in Crittenden county October 18 1867 a son of William W and Catherine Pogue Educated in public schools and Marion Academy and Normal School Married Miss Bettie F Matthews in 1887 Taught in the common schools for more than twenty years Member of 1902 House and Assistant Clerk of House 1903 1905 1907 Elected to present house over HE Worton Republican by 375 majority

Marion married **Bettie Florence Matthews** on 18 Apr 1887 in Crittenden County Kentucky.

Children from this marriage were:

3   i.   **Clara Augusta Pogue**

  ii.   **Forrest Carlisle Pogue Sr** was born on 20 Aug 1889 in Crittenden County Kentucky, died on 29 Oct 1946 in Crittenden County Kentucky at age 57, and was buried in Frances Presbyterian Church Cemetery Frances Crittenden County Kentucky.

M. F. Pogue

7. Bettie Florence Matthews, daughter of **John Matthews** and **Nancy M. Walker,** was born on 10 Nov 1868 in Crittenden County Kentucky, died on 29 Feb 1952 in Caldwell County Kentucky at age 83, and was buried in Frances Presbyterian Church Cemetery Frances Crittenden County Kentucky.

Bettie married **Marion Forrest Pogue** on 18 Apr 1887 in Crittenden County Kentucky.

Grave of Bettie Matthews Pouge

Fourth Generation (Great-Grandparents)

8. John Wesley Fox, son of **George Fox** and **Addy Jackson,** was born from circa 1815 to 1820 in Hamilton County Ohio and died after 1880 in Crittenden County Kentucky.

General Notes: Fox, John W.

Union

Cavalry

17th Regiment, Kentucky Cavalry

John married **Elizabeth King** circa 1842 in Hamilton County Ohio.

Children from this marriage were:

  i.   **William A. Fox** was born circa 1843 in Hamilton County Ohio.

  ii.   **Mary J. Fox** was born circa 1847 in Hamilton Cointy Ohio.

4   iii.   **Charles Wesley Fox**

John next married **Hannah Lawson** on 11 Mar 1869 in Hamilton County Ohio.

John next married **Ellen** circa 1877 in Crittenden County Kentucky.

9. Elizabeth King was born circa 1825 in Hamilton County Ohio and died before 1869 in Cincinnati, Hamilton County Ohio.

Elizabeth married **John Wesley Fox** circa 1842 in Hamilton County Ohio.

10. Asel Branson Hodge, son of **William Fidella Hodge** and **Nancy Josiphine Dancy,** was born on 18 Jan 1825 in Livingston County Kentucky and died on 4 Jan 1889 in Crittenden County Kentucky at age 63.

Asel married **Catharine Elizabeth Millikan**.

The child from this marriage was:

    5   i.   **Juliet Hodge**

Asel B. Hodge

11. Catharine Elizabeth Millikan, daughter of **Solomon Millikan** and **Nancy Morgan,** was born on 16 Oct 1829 in Grainger County Tennessee and died on 18 Dec 1889 in Crittenden County Kentucky at age 60.

Catharine married **Asel Branson Hodge**.

Catharine Elizabeth Millikan

12. William Washington Pogue, son of **Thomas Franklin Pogue** and **Harriet Cruise,** was born on 11 Dec 1845 in Murray, Calloway County, Kentucky, died on 5 Mar 1926 in Crittenden County Kentucky at age 80, and was buried in Oliver Cemetery.

William married **Mary Catherine Oliver** on 19 Dec 1866 in Crittenden County Kentucky.

The child from this marriage was:

    6   i.   **Marion Forrest Pogue**

Grave of William Washington Pogue

13. Mary Catherine Oliver, daughter of **Henry W. Oliver** and **Margaret C. Rolston,** was born on 22 Jul 1849 in Crittenden County Kentucky, died on 14 Apr 1939 in Crittenden County Kentucky at age 89, and was buried in Oliver Cemetery.

Mary married **William Washington Pogue** on 19 Dec 1866 in Crittenden County Kentucky.

Grave of Mary Catherine (Oliver) Pouge

14. John Matthews, son of **Joseph Matthews** and **Sarah Smith,** was born on 4 Jan 1824 in Livingston County Kentucky, died on 23 Aug 1910 in Crittenden County Kentucky at age 86, and was buried in Matthews Cemetery.

John married **Nancy M. Walker** on 1 Sep 1864 in Crittenden County Kentucky.

> Marriage Notes: Kentucky Marriages, 1851-1900 about Nancy M. Durham
> Name: John Matthews
> Spouse: Nancy M. Durham
> Marriage Date: 1 Sep 1864
> County: Crittenden
> State: KY

The child from this marriage was:

>   7   i.   **Bettie Florence Matthews**

15. Nancy M. Walker, daughter of **William E. Walker** and **Mary Fowler,** was born on 14 Nov 1835 in Tennessee, died on 30 Jun 1908 in Crittenden County Kentucky at age 72, and was buried in Matthews Cemetery.

Nancy married **John Matthews** on 1 Sep 1864 in Crittenden County Kentucky.

Nancy next married **Alfred Newton Durham** on 14 Nov 1847 in Christian County Kentucky.

Fifth Generation (Great Great-Grandparents)

16. George Fox, son of **Thomas Fox** and **Sarah Walker,** was born on 3 Sep 1775 in Finninlly, Yorkshire, , England and died on 16 Apr 1845 in Hamilton County Ohio at age 69.

> General Notes: Fox George, Millcreek Township 05/22/1845 Will Probated 2 Richard Fox John Fox, Richard Fox, Elisabeth Fox
>
> England & Wales Christening Records, 1530-1906 about George Foxx
> Name: George Foxx
> Gender: Male
> Birth Date: abt 1775
> Christening Date: 3 Sep 1775
> Christening Place: Finningley, Nottinghamshire, England
> Father's Name: Thomas Foxx
> Mother's name: Sarah

George married **Addy Jackson** on 14 Nov 1799 in Barnsley, Yorkshire, England.

Children from this marriage were:

George Fox

>   8   i.   **John Wesley Fox**
>
>   ii.   **Richard P. Fox** was born on 17 Nov 1805 in Arksey, Yorkshire, England and died on 8 Jan 1878 in Arcola, Douglas County, Illinois at age 72.
>
>   iii.   **Addy Jane Fox** was born in 1829 and died on 19 Mar 1889 in Cleveland, Cuyahoga County, Ohio at age 60.

17. Addy Jackson was born in 1775 and died on 4 Mar 1819 in Hamilton County Ohio at age 44.

Addy married **George Fox** on 14 Nov 1799 in Barnsley, Yorkshire, England.

20. William Fidella Hodge, son of **Henry Harry Hodge** and **Catherine Bryant,** was born in 1777 in Edgecombe County North Carolina and died in 1826 in Livingston County Kentucky at age 49.

William married **Nancy Josiphine Dancy**.

The child from this marriage was:

    10   i.   **Asel Branson Hodge**

21. Nancy Josiphine Dancy.

Nancy married **William Fidella Hodge**.

22. Solomon Millikan was born on 28 Feb 1784 in Grainger County Tennessee and died on 26 Oct 1860 in Crittenden County Kentucky at age 76.

Solomon married **Nancy Morgan** on 1 Aug 1804 in Grainger County Tennessee.

The child from this marriage was:

    11   i.   **Catharine Elizabeth Millikan**

Grave of Solomon & Nancy (Morgan) Millikan

23. Nancy Morgan was born in 1783 in Grainger County Tennessee and died in 1865 in Crittenden County Kentucky at age 82.

Nancy married **Solomon Millikan** on 1 Aug 1804 in Grainger County Tennessee.

24. Thomas Franklin Pogue, son of **William Thomas Pogue** and **Mary,** was born on 21 Jan 1802 in Tazwell County Virginia, died on 20 Jun 1857 in Calloway County, Kentucky at age 55, and was buried in Pogue Cemetery.

    General Notes: His death Record states Sabbed he was an Outlaw

Thomas married **Harriet Cruise** on 26 Dec 1844 in Graves County Kentucky.

The child from this marriage was:

    12   i.   **William Washington Pogue**

25. Harriet Cruise, daughter of **Jonathan Cruise** and **Holly Bennett,** was born on 11 May 1823 in North Carolina, died on 1 Dec 1892 in Calloway County, Kentucky at age 69, and was buried in Pogue Cemetery.

Harriet married **Thomas Franklin Pogue** on 26 Dec 1844 in Graves County Kentucky.

26. Henry W. Oliver, son of **Walter Oliver** and **Mary Cox Winn,** was born on 7 Oct 1816 in Virginia, died on 11 May 1873 in Crittenden County Kentucky at age 56, and was buried in Oliver Cemetery.

Henry married **Margaret C. Rolston** on 2 Sep 1847 in Trigg County Kentucky.

The child from this marriage was:

    13   i.   **Mary Catherine Oliver**

Grave of Hery W. Oliver

27. Margaret C. Rolston, daughter of **William Rolston** and **Catherine Chisman,** was born on 6 Jan 1823 in Trigg County Kentucky, died on 27 Nov 1892 in Crittenden County Kentucky at age 69, and was buried in Oliver Cemetery.

Margaret married **Henry W. Oliver** on 2 Sep 1847 in Trigg County Kentucky.

Grave of Margaret Rolston Oliver

28. Joseph Matthews.

Joseph married **Sarah Smith.**

The child from this marriage was:

    14   i.   **John Matthews**

29. Sarah Smith was born in 1778 in North Carolina, died on 29 Oct 1873 in Crittenden County Kentucky at age 95, and was buried in Matthews Cemetery.

Sarah married **Joseph Matthews.**

30. William E. Walker.

William married **Mary Fowler.**

The child from this marriage was:

    15   i.   **Nancy M. Walker**

31. Mary Fowler.

Mary married **William E. Walker**.

Sixth Generation (3rd Great-Grandparents)

32. Thomas Fox, son of **William Fox** and **Hannah Ann Shepherd,** was born circa 1739 in Doncaster, Yorkshire, England, was christened on 6 May 1739 in Hatfield, Doncaster, Yorkshire, England, died on 19 Sep 1801 in Finningley, Yorkshire, England about age 62, and was buried in Holy Trinity & St. Oswald/St. Saviour.

Thomas married **Sarah Walker** on 14 Jun 1767 in Yorkshire, England.

Children from this marriage were:

    16   i.   **George Fox**

           ii.   **Richard Fox**

         iii.   **Thomas Fox**

         iv.   **John Fox**

Holy Trinity & St. Oswald

33. Sarah Walker, daughter of **Richard Walker** and **Mary Freeman,** was born in 1742 in Fishlake, Yorkshire, England, was christened on 28 Dec 1742 in Fishlake, Yorkshire, England, died on 19 Jun 1827 in Finningley, Yorkshire, England at age 85, and was buried in Holy Trinity & St. Oswald/St. Saviour.

Sarah married **Thomas Fox** on 14 Jun 1767 in Yorkshire, England.

Grave of Thomas Fox

40. Henry Harry Hodge, son of **John or Johnson Hodge** and **Mary,** was born circa 1745 in North Carolina and died on 10 Feb 1824 in Livingston County Kentucky about age 79.

Henry married **Catherine Bryant** before 1777.

The child from this marriage was:

    20   i.   **William Fidella Hodge**

41. Catherine Bryant was born in 1752 in North Carolina and died circa 1794 in Livingston County Kentucky about age 42.

Catherine married **Henry Harry Hodge** before 1777.

48. William Thomas Pogue, son of **Col. William Pogue (Poage)** and **Margaret Davies,** was born on 8 Feb 1783 in Pocahontas County Virginia now West Virginia and died on 27 May 1827 in Tazwell County Virginia at age 44.

William married **Mary**.

Children from this marriage were:

    24   i.   **Thomas Franklin Pogue**

ii.   **Hiram Pogue** was born about 1814 in Virginia.

49. Mary was born in 1784 in Virginia.

Mary married **William Thomas Pogue**.

50. Jonathan Cruise was born circa 1790 in Greenville County South Carolina and died in Oct 1864 in Crittenden County Kentucky about age 74.

Jonathan married **Holly Bennett**.

The child from this marriage was:

25   i.   **Harriet Cruise**

51. Holly Bennett was born about 1794 in Madison County Kentucky and died before 1850 in Calloway County Kentucky.

Holly married **Jonathan Cruise**.

52. Walter Oliver.

Walter married **Mary Cox Winn**.

The child from this marriage was:

26   i.   **Henry W. Oliver**

53. Mary Cox Winn.

Mary married **Walter Oliver**.

54. William Rolston.

William married **Catherine Chisman**.

The child from this marriage was:

27   i.   **Margaret C. Rolston**

55. Catherine Chisman.

Catherine married **William Rolston**.

Seventh Generation (4th Great-Grandparents)

64. William Fox, son of **Thomas Fox** and **Elizabeth Renneson,** was born about 1679 in Yorkshire, England and died on 25 Dec 1741 in Doncaster, Yorkshire, England about age 62.

General Notes: 1670s Britain's oldest foxhunt, the Bilsdale in Yorkshire, founded

William married **Hannah Ann Shepherd**.

The child from this marriage was:

32   i.   **Thomas Fox**

65. Hannah Ann Shepherd, daughter of **Bryan Shepherd** and **Elizabeth Becket,** was born in 1698 in Barnsley, St Mary, Yorkshire, England and was christened on 1 May 1698 in Barnsley, St Mary, Yorkshire, England.

Hannah married **William Fox**.

66. Richard Walker.

Richard married **Mary Freeman**.

The child from this marriage was:

33   i.   **Sarah Walker**

67. Mary Freeman.

Mary married **Richard Walker**.

80. John or Johnson Hodge, son of **Thomas Hodge** and **Christian Woodson,** was born in 1709 in Cumberland County Virginia and died in 1773 in Augusta County, Virginia at age 64.

> General Notes: Thomas Hodges who wrote his will in 1749 probated in 1750 in Cumberland Co., Va. (made from Goochland Co., Va.) Abstract of Thomas Hodges will names Christian (his wife) and William Womack as co-executors and makes bequests to his children William, John, Drury, Thomas, Edmund, Mary, and Delany. Witnessed by Henry Bell, John Chafin, and William Mills. An interesting tidbit is that T. Hodges also knew the Governor Richard Bennett excerpt from his will as follows (...Lastly, I do hereby declare and ordain and appoint James Jofey, Mr. Thomas Hodges, and Edmond Belson or any two of them also Robert Pealle to be overseers of this my last will and testament allowing & approving for good and effectual to all intents and purposes what so ever my said executors or any two of them shall do or cause to be done concerning the estate from time to time in relation to the estate.) Thomas Hodges was also one of the witnesses to the marriage of Edmond Belson son of Elizabeth Belson of Nansemond Co. to Mary Crew, daughter of Mary Took of Isle of Wight Co. on 13 Nov. 1684 I Valentine Papers 210, (from the records of to Society of Friends, Lower Virginia Meeting).
>
> Edmund Hodges was next in my line. With Edmund we have a good deal of data that exists today. Edmund performed the patriotic service of furnishing supplies for the soldiers during the Revolutionary War. (Source: Hodges Notes Hart Co. Historical Society from Chatham, Va. courthouse.)
> Abstra ct of Edmund Hodges Will it reads in part:
> (...I Edmund Hodges of the County of Pittsylvania... lend to my loving wife Nephany during her natural life or widowhood my whole estate...
> ...to my five sons John Hodges, Thomas Hodges, Moses Hodges, David Hodges, and Jesse Hodges eight hundred acres of land to be divided amongst them so that my son Thomas have is land where I now dwell and my son David to have his land taking the place where Samuel Morley (Mosley sp?) did settle on and if it please God to take me out of this world before I do clear out the survey that was surveyed for me adjoining the patton (pattern?) land the money to be paid out of my estate for the clearing the land out of the office...) This will lists wife and 5 boys. And later in a codicil we find a daughter Susannah Hodges. This daughter married a John Slayden, there is some question as to exact spelling of his name, but I will use Slayden here. (In a codicil dated 11 Feb 1782 and witnessed by Joseph Akin, William Briswell, and Robert Hopper
> ...My daughter Susannah Slayton's equal part of my moveabel Estate which I do hereby revoke and disannul as she has since deceased. I do will and bequeath the same part of my moveable estate which was allotted to her to be equally divided amongst her six children viz: James, Rachel, Pattsey, John, Edmund, and Arthur Porter Slayton....) Here we have what looks to be a sad event, a daughter passing on. I still haven't a clear mind on Edmund there is still some data that does not all fit. From my aunt Geraldine Hodges I have her saying Edmund was a "native of Ireland... migrating to America and settling in Virginia." The research I have does not fit exactly with this thought. Edmund although not a common name does appear in more than one place. I feel he is the Edmund of Goochland Co.This deed mentions Edmund. .Joseph Scott of Goochland Co. sold 20 A ... Lickinghole Creek to Edmund Hodges... Joseph Scott of Amelia Co. sold to Henry Wood ... 400 A on the North side of James Rive... Lickinghole Creek, excepting 20 A conveyed to Edmund Hodges. Our Edmund marry's Nephanah Walker and has 9 children. They were married in St James Northam Parish, in Goochland Co. The church in the 1700's was of great importance in people's lives. Birth's, death's, social events, everyone went to the church, they were the hub along with the town, which peoples lives were intertwined.

John married **Mary**.

The child from this marriage was:

    40   i.   **Henry Harry Hodge**

81. Mary.

Mary married **John or Johnson Hodge**.

96. Col. William Pogue (Poage), son of **John Pogue (Poage)** and **Mary Blair Crawford,** was born on 17 Feb 1756 in Augusta County, Virginia and died on 7 Apr 1830 in Pocahontas County Virginia now West Virginia at age 74.

William married **Margaret Davies**.

The child from this marriage was:

    48   i.   **William Thomas Pogue**

97. Margaret Davies was born in 1749 in Augusta County Virginia and died in 1843 in Pocahontas County Virginia now West Virginia at age 94.

Margaret married **Col. William Pogue (Poage)**.

Eighth Generation (5th Great-Grandparents)

128. Thomas Fox, son of **Thomas Fox** and **Unknown,** was born circa 1618 in Allhallowes in Northstret, Yorkshire England and died circa 1680 in Yorkshire England about age 62.

    General Notes: From Doncaster Parish Ye Tms Fox died 1680

Thomas married **Elizabeth Renneson** on 8 Aug 1658 in St. Michaels in Yorkshire.

The child from this marriage was:

    64   i.   **William Fox**

129. Elizabeth Renneson was born circa 1625 in Bellfriraies, Yorkshire England.

Elizabeth married **Thomas Fox** on 8 Aug 1658 in St. Michaels in Yorkshire.

130. Bryan Shepherd.

Bryan married **Elizabeth Becket** on 8 Jun 1697 in Barnsley, Yorkshire, England.

The child from this marriage was:

    65   i.   **Hannah Ann Shepherd**

131. Elizabeth Becket.

Elizabeth married **Bryan Shepherd** on 8 Jun 1697 in Barnsley, Yorkshire, England.

160. Thomas Hodge, son of **Thomas Hodge** and **Charity Ramsey,** was born on 3 Nov 1697 in Anne Arundel County, Maryland and died circa 1731 in Goochland County , Virginia about age 34.

Thomas married **Christian Woodson** circa 1705 in Virginia.

The child from this marriage was:

    80   i.   **John or Johnson Hodge**

161. Christian Woodson was born in 1681 in Cumberland County Virginia and died circa 1713 in Goochland County, Virginia about age 32.

Christian married **Thomas Hodge** circa 1705 in Virginia.

192. John Pogue (Poage), son of **Robert Pogue (Poage)** and **Elizabeth Preston,** was born about 1726 in Ireland and died circa 1789 in Augusta County, Virginia about age 63.

John married **Mary Blair Crawford** on 3 Jun 1751 in Augusta County, Virginia.

The child from this marriage was:

    96   i.   **Col. William Pogue (Poage)**

193. Mary Blair Crawford was born circa 1725 in Drumore Township, Lancaster, Pennsylvania, USA and died after 1789 in Augusta County, Virginia.

Mary married **John Pogue (Poage)** on 3 Jun 1751 in Augusta County, Virginia.

Ninth Generation (6th Great-Grandparents)

256. Thomas Fox, son of **Thomas Fox** and **(Isabell),** was born in 1593 in Yorkshire England, was christened on 13 Jul 1593 in Askham Yorkshire England, and died on 5 Nov 1624 in Yorkshire England at age 31.

Thomas married someone.

His children were:

> 128   i.   **Thomas Fox**
>
>   ii.   **Jonathan Fox** was born circa 1620 in Yorkshire England.
>
>   iii.   **John Fox** was born circa 1622.

320. Thomas Hodge, son of **Humphrey Hodge** and **Mary Anderson,** was born on 15 Sep 1671 in Anna Arundel County, Maryland and died circa 1731 in Anna Arundel County, Maryland about age 60.

> General Notes: Thomas Barnes, son of Humphrey and Mary, was born 15 September 1671. He arrived in Pennsylvania with his mother and stepfather on 20 August 1683. Although there are one or two Thomas Hodges appearing in the records of Philadelphia Meetings, Kenneth Hodges advances compelling reasons why the Thomaas who married Charity Ramsey may well have left the Quaker fold and become Episcopalian. On 13 May 1697 he witnessed the will of John Belt of Anne Arundel Co. Thomas disappeared from Maryland records after the death of Charity (who died before 1714).

Thomas married **Charity Ramsey** circa 1696 in Anna Arundel County, Maryland.

The child from this marriage was:

> 160   i.   **Thomas Hodge**

321. Charity Ramsey was born circa 1684 in Anna Arundel County, Maryland and died circa 1714 in Anna Arundel County, Maryland about age 30.

Charity married **Thomas Hodge** circa 1696 in Anna Arundel County, Maryland.

384. Robert Pogue (Poage) was born circa 1699 in Ireland and died circa 1732 in Augusta County, Virginia about age 33.

Robert married **Elizabeth Preston** circa 1722 in Ireland.

The child from this marriage was:

> 192   i.   **John Pogue (Poage)**

385. Elizabeth Preston.

Elizabeth married **Robert Pogue (Poage)** circa 1722 in Ireland.

Tenth Generation (7th Great-Grandparents)

512. Thomas Fox, son of **Johes Fox** and **Isabella Hawen,** was born in 1567, was christened on 2 Jan 1568 in Huddersfield, St Peter, and died on 18 Jan 1638 in Askham Yorkshire England at age 71.

> General Notes: Yorkshire: Allerton Mauleverer (1562-1812), Askham Richard (1578-1762 - Parish Registers (Christenings, Marriages, Burials)

Thomas married **(Isabell)**.

Children from this marriage were:

> 256   i.   **Thomas Fox**
>
>   ii.   **Richard Fox** was born in 1597.

513. (Isabell) died on 5 Dec 1627 in Askham Yorkshire England.

> General Notes: States her death date but not her name

(Isabell) married **Thomas Fox.**

640. Humphrey Hodge, son of **Captain John Twigg Hodge** and **Mary Miller,** was born circa 1623 in Charlestown, Middlesex County, Massachusetts and died in 1680 in Barbados about age 57.

> General Notes: Persecution as Quaker

The first meeting of Friends in Boston, of which we have account, was at the house of Mr. Wanton, on the 4th of May, when a warrant was issued to apprehend the preacher, and report the names of his hearers to the governour. The spirit of persecution was kept alive and manifested itself in various ways, after this. On the 9ih of August, l675, there were dQuakers apprehended, at their ordinary place of meeting, Kobt. Edmund, Edw. Shippen, John Soames, Jere. Debee, Geo. Danson, Miles Foster, Humphrey Hodges, Bridget Phillips, Thos. Scott, Wm. Nrlal, Eph. Stratton, Elizabeth Bowers (senior and junior), Geo. Walker. Twelve of these 14 were whipped ; the other two paid their fines.

from A History of Boston: The Metropolis of Massachusetts by Caleb Hopkins Snow - 1828 - Boston (Mass.)

Humphrey married **Mary Anderson** circa 1663 in Middlesex County Mass.

The child from this marriage was:

    320   i.   **Thomas Hodge**

641. Mary Anderson was born circa 1638 in Middlesex County Mass.

Mary married **Humphrey Hodge** circa 1663 in Middlesex County Mass.

11th Generation (8th Great-Grandparents)

1024. Johes Fox, son of **Edmund Edmundus Fox** and **Susanna,** was born in 1541, was christened on 4 Dec 1541 in Kirkburton, All Hallows Yorkshire England, and died on 1 Jan 1578 in Huddersfield, St Peter Yorkshire England at age 37.

Johes married **Isabella Hawen** on 19 Jun 1569 in Halifax, All Souls, Haley Hill Yorkshire England.

    Marriage Notes: She may be a secod wife

The child from this marriage was:

    512   i.   **Thomas Fox**

1025. Isabella Hawen.

Isabella married **Johes Fox** on 19 Jun 1569 in Halifax, All Souls, Haley Hill Yorkshire England.

1280. Captain John Twigg Hodge, son of **Humphrey Twigg Hodge** and **Margaret Timperly,** was born in 1600 in Wapping, Middlesex, England and died on 10 Oct 1654 in Charlestown, Suffolk County, Massachusetts at age 54.

    General Notes: In November, 1633, the Rebecca, of about 60 tons, was built at Medford, Mass., for Gov. Matthew Cradock and his partners, and William Pierce was given command. Perhaps John Hodges was mate. We know that on Dec. 18, 1634, the Rebecca, Capt. William Pierce, sailed from Massachusetts for England; and on April 6 and 9, 1635, the Rebecca, Capt. John Hodges, was at London taking passengers and freight for New England. In 1635 and 1636 John Hodges was making constant trips in the Rebecca, plying between Boston and Connecticut, with letters and commissions of Gov. John Winthrop, senior, of Massachusetts and Gov. John Winthrop, junior, of Connecticut, going north to the Isle of Sable for sea-horse and cows, and south to Bermuda, whence he returned with "30,000 weight of potatoes and store of oranges and limes." Early in 1637 Matthew Cradock in London wrote to Gov. Winthrop in Boston, directing that John Hodges should resume command of the Rebecca and take this ship with her "ordynance," and victualled for three months, to Virginia. Why "resume" is not stated, nor whether John Hodges and the Rebecca made this voyage.

    kathilieoriginally submitted this to Hodges-Boles-Gruggett-Flores on 11 Sep 2009

John married **Mary Miller** circa 1617 in Middlesex County Massachusetts.

The child from this marriage was:

    640   i.   **Humphrey Hodge**

1281. Mary Miller was born in 1605 in Charlestown, Middlesex County, Massachusetts and died on 11 Mar 1693 in Boston Suffolk County Massachusetts at age 88.

Mary married **Captain John Twigg Hodge** circa 1617 in Middlesex County Massachusetts.

12th Generation (9th Great-Grandparents)

2048. Edmund Edmundus Fox was born in Yorkshire: Dewsbury - Parish Registers Yorkshire England.

Edmund married **Susanna**.

Children from this marriage were:

    1024   i.   **Johes Fox**

          ii.   **Edmundus Fox** died on 14 Oct 1577 in Halifax, All Souls, Haley Hill Yorkshire England.

          iii. **Johanna Fox** was born in 1548.

2049. Susanna died on 15 Jan 1565 in Dewsbury Yorkshire West Ridings, England and was buried in St John the Baptist, Yorkshire, England.

Susanna married **Edmund Edmundus Fox**.

2560. Humphrey Twigg Hodge was born in 1584 in Derbyshire, England and died on 28 Feb 1624 in Derbyshire, England at age 40.

Humphrey married **Margaret Timperly** on 12 May 1604 in Youlgreave, Derbyshire, England.

The child from this marriage was:

    1280   i.   **Captain John Twigg Hodge**

2561. Margaret Timperly was born in 1584 in Ashbourne, Derbyshire, England and died on 28 Feb 1624 in Youlgreave, Derbyshire, England at age 40.

Margaret married **Humphrey Twigg Hodge** on 12 May 1604 in Youlgreave, Derbyshire, England.

Name Index

Name Index

Davies

    Margaret, 26, 28

Davis

    Charles, 8

    John M., 7, 8, 12

    Mary Elizabeth, 6, 7, 8

    Moses, 11, 14, 17

    Robert, 14, 17

    Thomas, 8, 11, 12, 14

Durham

    Alfred Newton, 23

Fowler

    Mary, 23, 25

    Roseannah, 9, 12, 13, 14

Fox

    Addy Jane, 23

    Charles Wesley, 20, 21

    Edmund Edmundus, 31, 32

    Edmundus, 32

    George, 21, 23, 24, 26

    Johanna, 32

    Johes, 30, 31, 32

    John, 26, 30

    John Wesley, 20, 21, 22, 23

    Jonathan, 30

    Marian Verna, 1, 5, 19, 20

    Mary J., 21

    Richard, 26, 30

    Richard P., 23

    Richard Wesley, 20

    Thelma N., 20

    Thomas, 23, 26, 27, 29, 30, 31

    Vernon Richard, 1, 5, 19, 20

    William, 26, 27, 29

    William A., 21

    William Garrad, 20

Franklin

    Leah Michelle, 4

    Robert Michael, 3, 4

Freeman

    Mary, 26, 27

Name Index

Name Index

Name Index

Name Index

www.ingramcontent.com/pod-product-compliance
Lightning Source LLC
Chambersburg PA
CBHW060836290526
45792CB00006BB/1948